9·25·79

UNDERSTANDING TODAY'S ECONOMICS

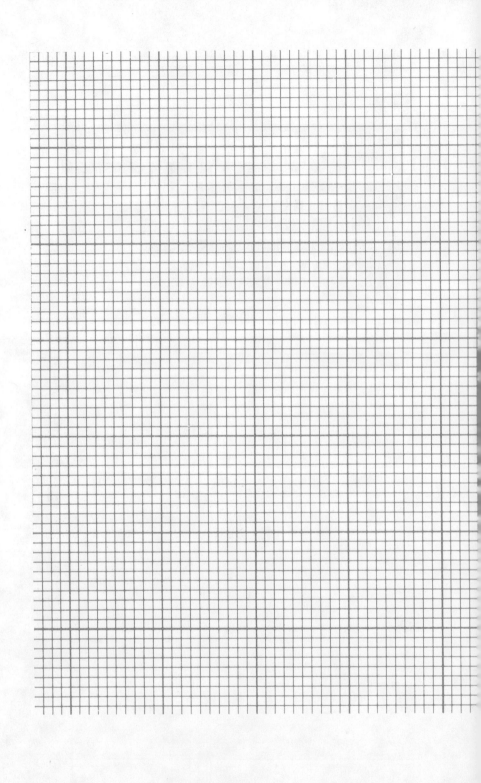

UNDER-STANDING TODAY'S ECONOMICS

BY ROBERT CRANE

FRANKLIN WATTS
NEW YORK | LONDON | 1979
AN IMPACT BOOK

Photographs courtesy of:
The Bettmann Archive: pp. 9, 50; United Press International: p. 55; The New York Stock Exchange: p. 58; Commodities Exchange Center, Inc.: p. 61.

Art Courtesy of: Vantage Art, Inc.

Library of Congress Cataloging in Publication Data

Crane, Robert, 1938–
Understanding today's economics.

(An impact book)
Bibliography: p.
Includes index.
SUMMARY: Discusses the basic elements of economics in a capitalist system and explains how they interrelate with each other.

1. Economics—Juvenile literature. [1. Economics]
I. Title.
HB171.7.C7943   330   78–11536
ISBN 0–531–02285–4

CONTENTS

2065854

UNDERSTANDING TODAY'S ECONOMICS

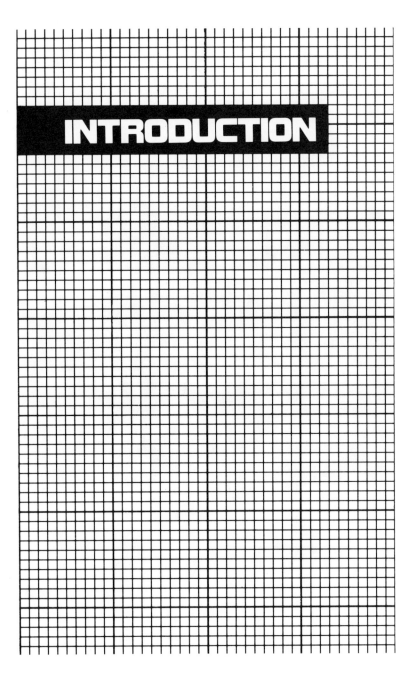

INTRODUCTION

Of all the sciences, only two can really be said to deal with subjects that have a very direct and perceptible impact on the lives of every one of us each and every day.

One is meteorology, the study of weather. Whether it is hot or cold, whether it will be rainy or sunny will affect us in many ways—the kind of clothing we will wear and the types of activities we will engage in outdoors, for example.

Economics is the other science that affects the everyday lives of us all, although we may not be fully aware of it. Each time we spend money, or it is spent on our behalf, whatever amount it may be, we are contributing to the economic life of our country, and, in fact, of the world.

In a sense, we are all amateur meteorologists. We can feel the heat and the cold. We can appreciate a clear, beautiful day. We can look at a darkening sky and conclude that it will rain.

Economics is different. None of us, aside from the professional economist, feels really comfortable with the subject. Prices go up. The factory that employs one of our relatives or friends closes temporarily. The interest rate on our bank savings account drops. We notice each of these events and others of a similar nature and wonder why these things happen.

Economics does seem to be a darkly mysterious subject. The news publications and the television news programs discuss the topic in terminology that seems as indecipherable as a remote foreign language. They speak of the gross national product, the cost of living, the prime rate, the money supply, productivity, the unemployment rate, the balance of payments. You may justifiably wonder what it all means and how it all fits together, if indeed it does.

[3]

In some ways, economics is like an enormous jig-saw puzzle. When the pieces are dumped out of the box and scattered across the table, the job of putting them all together may seem very difficult. The only way to proceed from the scattered pile to a finished puzzle is to take one piece at a time, become familiar with its contours, and then find the piece that matches it.

The terms we used before (and all the other phrases used in economics) are very much like the pieces of a jigsaw puzzle, each of them with a different shape, or meaning. If you could fit them all together easily, you would qualify as a first-rate economist.

The apparent incomprehensibility of economics can be overcome by developing an understanding of the very basic elements of the science and learning how they interrelate, one to another. As dry as the subject may seem, it is in fact fascinating once you begin to fit the pieces together.

PRODUCTION

If economics is like a giant jigsaw puzzle, where do we begin? Theoretically, a jigsaw puzzle can be started with any piece. If you have done a puzzle before, however, you know that the best way to begin is with the border pieces. Find a corner piece and then match up the straight-sided pieces until the border is completed and the outer edges are in place. After that, you work inward toward the center.

Economics, too, has a set of border pieces. They were provided over 200 years ago by a man named Adam Smith, a Scotsman and a social philosopher. In 1776, two events of historical importance occurred. The United States was born as an independent nation. In perspective, it was an event that would overshadow anything else that occurred that year. But 1776 was also notable in that it was the year in which modern economics was born. The publication of Adam Smith's *The Wealth of Nations* was responsible for the start of the new science.

The principles Adam Smith laid down in his book were not discoveries in the sense that they revealed something previously unknown. Many of Adam Smith's principles were known, at least intuitively, by people who lived before him. What made his work extraordinary was that he systematized the principles of economics and explained how they interrelated with one another. In effect, Adam Smith did for economics what Einstein did for the science of nuclear physics.

To fully appreciate Adam Smith's accomplishment, one must understand something of the times in which he lived. In the late 1700s, the world was moving slowly, almost grudgingly, toward the Industrial Age. Individual handwork remained the process by which most products were made, and the artisans of the time usually worked their products from beginning to end. A plow, for example, might have been produced by one person who shaped the handles from raw wood, forged the cutting edge from iron, and then bound the two elements together.

That practice was just beginning to change. The textile industry was one major business field that was mechanizing. Factories were springing up in that industry, and mass production was becoming more and more commonplace in Adam Smith's lifetime. It was from the textile industry and related manufacturing that Adam Smith formulated most of his principles as they apply to modern economics.

The first principle he explained in *The Wealth of Nations* was the **division of labor,** as he called it. It is quite logically first because it is upon this principle that industrialization rests.

This principle is relatively simple. It says that by dividing the production of a manufactured item among the workers, and assigning each to a specific part of the operation, production can be vastly increased over the output that would be possible if each worker were responsible for production of an item from beginning to end.

DIVISION OF LABOR

Adam Smith used pin manufacturing as an example, which should not be surprising, because the growth of the textile industry in the 1700s had created an enormous demand for pins for sewing. It made the old practice of producing pins by hand totally impractical, forcing mass production techniques on the industry.

Adam Smith watched the pin-making business

**Adam Smith, author of _The_
Wealth of Nations, in 1790.**

adapt to the upsurge in demand and was inspired by the new efficiencies that were introduced. Here is how he described the industry's mass production techniques as compared with the older methods.

One man draws out the wire, another straightens it, a third cuts it, a fourth points it, a fifth grinds it at the top for receiving the head; to make the head requires three distinct operations; to put it on is a peculiar [meaning "special"] business, to whiten the pins is another; it is even a trade by itself to put them into the paper; and the important business of making a pin is, in this manner, divided into about eighteen distinct operations, which, in some manufactories, are all performed by distinct hands, though in others the same man will sometimes perform two or three of them.

He noted that he had seen small pin-making operations where ten workers could make up to 48,000 pins a day because of the division of labor. He added that if they had all worked independently of one another, each responsible for the entire process, "they could certainly not each of them have made twenty, perhaps not one pin in a day."

We cannot underestimate the importance of this principle in the making of our modern industrial world. Without the division of labor, today's standard of living would have been impossible. (Economics professors, incidentally, often cannot resist the temptation to tell their students that it was Adam Smith who "pinpointed" the principle.)

The modern version of the division of labor can be seen in the assembly line, where workers usually stay in one place and the product, in its various stages of manufacturing, moves to them. The best example of this is in the automotive industry. As the components of a car move along the assembly line, one group of workers will bolt on the front bumper; the next might fasten the tail lights; the next, the windshield wipers; and so on.

In this manner, cars can be mass produced. If one worker had the responsibility for every facet of production, working on only one car at a time, the worker might be lucky to complete one automobile a year. By comparison, the Japanese, who have become most efficient at automobile production, turn out an average of about 35 cars a year per worker.

PRODUCTIVITY

This leads us to a widely misunderstood term—**productivity.** The definition of productivity is simply the value of goods or services produced by a worker in a given period of time, be it a month or a year. The Japanese autoworker's productivity in a year is 35 cars multiplied by the monetary value of the average Japanese car.

The productivity for an entire nation can be determined by taking the estimated value of all goods and services produced in, say, a year (the **gross national product,** or **GNP,** as it is abbreviated) and dividing it by the number of workers. This would give you the productivity of each person in the working force. By itself, that figure wouldn't really mean a lot, unless you wanted to compare the productivity of different countries.

It is of its greatest value when productivity figures are compared from one year to the next. The movement up or down can be very significant because it indicates something about the economic health of a country. There is a direct link between changes in the rate of productivity and the national standard of living. If wages are increased, the cost of producing goods goes up. If worker productivity, however, rises at about the same rate, it balances off the increase in wages and keeps the cost of each product manufactured at about the same level. The manufacturer doesn't have to raise prices, and the workers have more money to spend.

From 1950 to 1970, the productivity of American workers roughly doubled. Over that period, the **real wages** (after inflation had been taken into consideration) also doubled for the average American worker. That means that the U.S. worker had twice as much money to spend in 1970 as he or she had in 1950, even considering the fact that prices rose quite a bit in that 20-year period.

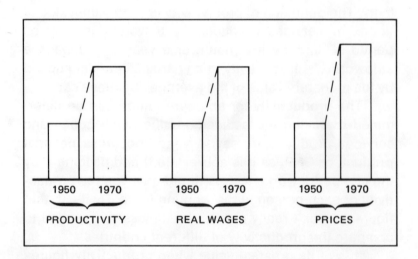

We mentioned earlier that productivity is a widely misunderstood term. When people read statements in the press that improvements in productivity are necessary for the well-being of the nation's economy, many take it to mean that everyone should work harder. That isn't entirely true.

Improved productivity is only partially due to a willingness to exert oneself more on the job. A more important part of the equation is the efficiency of the workplace and the equipment used in the production of goods and services.

Let's go back to Adam Smith's pin factory for a moment. He cited the case of a factory where ten workers were able to produce 48,000 pins a day. If the ten were working at their maximum speed to produce that quantity of pins, nothing could be done to improve productivity unless some new efficiency were found for the manufacturing process. After all, if the workers were going at full speed, that's as much as can be expected of them.

But suppose someone invents a machine that does some of the more time-consuming parts of their jobs. The additional time they had available could be devoted to greater production. Their productivity would rise.

THE ROLE OF CAPITAL

A good part of the responsibility for higher productivity falls to company management. If management continually provides more efficient machinery, workers are increasingly capable of higher productivity. This is the role of capital in production.

The word **capital** is most commonly associated with money in economic usage. Actually, it is applied more broadly than that. It actually stands for the means of production. Capital is money, yes; but it is also the machinery and equipment used in production, the plant

[13]

that houses the machinery and equipment, and other things. Some industries are referred to as **capital intensive.** This means that they require an expensive plant, machinery, and equipment for production. The steel industry is an example. Other industries are called **labor intensive,** meaning that wages represent the larger share of the cost of production. The fast-food industry is one example. Some industries cannot be so easily classified because their capital and labor requirements may be of relatively equal importance.

Money to pay for the means of production is obtained by a company in several ways. At the outset, when a company is being formed, the owners will invest their money in it so that the company can purchase what it needs to start operations and will have enough additional money, **working capital,** to pay the costs of operating. A company may also borrow money from a bank or some other lending institution in order to help pay for the means of production, or later for expansion.

PRICES AND PROFITS

Once a company is in operation, however, the principal source of money for improving productivity should be the revenues it receives for the sale of its goods or services. The price a company charges for its products or services must be based on careful consideration of a number of factors. First of all, the average price charged must be sufficient to cover all costs, including those for production, shipping, selling, and so forth. On top of that, prices must be sufficiently high to provide the company with a profit.

The concept of **profit** is frequently very much misunderstood. Studies have shown that the American public does not really understand the importance of business profits for the well-being of our free enterprise economy.

We earlier spoke of the importance of productivity, stating that improvement in productivity is directly connected to betterment of society's standard of living. Business profitability and improved productivity are very closely connected concepts.

A dictionary definition of the word *profit* is "financial gain resulting from the use of capital in a transaction." But a definition of profit gives only half the story. What profit is used for and where it goes are equally important concepts.

CORPORATE TAXES

The biggest share of most large companies' profits goes to the U.S. government in **taxes.** The tax rate on profits of large corporations is 48 percent. That means that the federal government takes almost half of corporate profits. What is left, on average, is about five or six cents out of every dollar of sales. Out of that amount, many companies pay a sum of money to the owners—the companies' **shareholders**—as dividends. A **dividend** is the owners' share in the profitability of the company. The profits after taxes must also provide the money a company needs for expansion or for improvements in production processes.

And here is where productivity comes back into the picture. If a company's productivity remained steady over a period of years, there could be adverse consequences. If production costs were rising—because of higher wages for workers and higher prices for equipment and raw materials—these additional costs would have to be passed on to the company's customers through higher prices. If this were happening throughout the economy—little or no productivity gains—most companies would be raising prices. **Inflation** would occur, and everyone would lose. Workers would be getting higher pay, but they would also be paying higher prices for the things they needed. Businesses would be similarly hurt.

The simplest way to improve productivity and avoid the necessity of raising prices when costs go up is to make production more efficient. Better machinery may accomplish this goal on a production line.

To illustrate the importance of profits, let's say that ten years ago the Jones Company purchased $100,000 worth of machinery for its production line. Today, the machinery has reached the end of its useful life. It is no longer functioning as well as it once did, and the company's efficiency is declining, which means worker productivity is going down.

The $100,000 cost of the machinery was taken into consideration in the pricing of the Jones Company's products. Over the past ten years, the company has been, in effect, setting aside $10,000 a year for replacement of the machinery.

In the meantime, there has been a very substantial inflation during the last ten years. Replacing the machinery with something very similar might now cost $150,000. Where will the extra $50,000 come from? It must be provided out of profits.

But suppose the Jones Company's owners decide that to improve productivity they need bigger and better machinery. And let's suppose that better machinery costs $250,000. Where does the extra $150,000 come from? It must come out of profits.

Profits are also the source of money for business expansion. If businesses didn't expand, the entire economy would be in trouble. In the first place, as the population increases, the work force grows. The number of young people entering the job market rises faster than the rate of worker retirement. Without business expansion, there would be no new jobs to fill, and the number of people unable to find work would steadily rise.

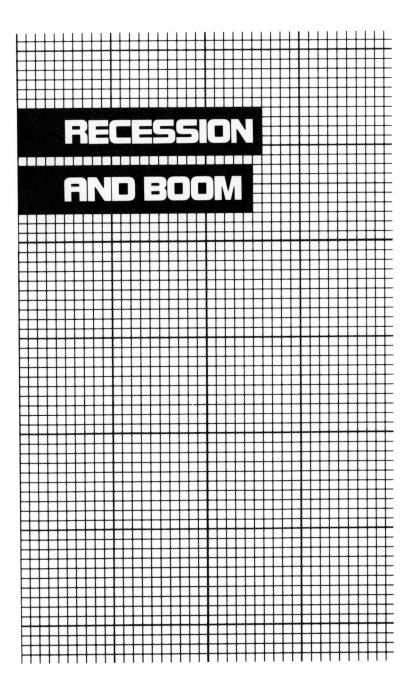

RECESSION AND BOOM

One of the principles set down by Adam Smith in *The Wealth of Nations* describes what has come to be known as the **law of supply and demand.** In simplified terms, he explained that when demand exceeds the supply of a product, those who want it tend to get into a bidding competition with one another, thus driving the price up. Conversely, when the supply of a product is higher than the demand for it, the seller tends to reduce the price in an attempt to encourage purchase of the product.

LAW OF SUPPLY AND DEMAND

Our entire free enterprise economy perches rather precariously on this principle. The ideal goal would be to keep these two forces—supply and demand—in balance. Unfortunately, that is not easy. In fact, it is actually impossible, given the fact that millions of products and services are on the market in an economy as diverse and complicated as ours is, since perfect balance would require that the supply and demand factors affecting each and every one of them be in true harmony.

The law of supply and demand affects the general economy in two significant ways. First, an imbalance impacts upon the health of the economy. Secondly, it has direct bearing on the overall level of prices.

Looking at the economy as a whole, if supply of goods and services exceeds demand, production has to be slowed down to give demand an opportunity to digest the excess supply. This can lead to **recession.**

On the other hand, if demand is higher than supply, the competitive bidding element enters the equation, and prices are driven up, causing inflation.

BUSINESS CYCLES

Because it is impossible to really balance supply and demand forces in our free enterprise economy, we experience ups and downs in business. For a while, business will be generally good, factories will be humming, and employment will be high. Then business activity will decline, factories will shut down or reduce their output, and a relatively high number of people will be unemployed. This whole process is called the **business cycle.**

In the 1960s, when the United States was experiencing a prolonged period of general business health, some economists convinced themselves that the business cycle was a thing of the past. Then came the recession that began in 1969, which was followed by a recovery that started in 1972, which in turn was followed by another recession beginning in 1975. Instead of claiming that business cycles have been eliminated, economists are trying to figure out why the cycles seem to have gotten shorter.

Business cycles remain one of the great mysteries of economics. Economists have many different theories about how to deal with them, but no one can say for certain why they occur or how they start. Our economy is so complex that we may in fact never be able to fully understand them.

As a general rule, however, recessions start with a slackening of demand, but not necessarily for all prod-

**Low prices and high demand
are good economic signs.
But high prices and low
demand lead to bad times.**

ucts or even a majority of products. If a few key industries experience a slackening of demand, it can have an effect like a stone tossed into a quiet pond; the ripples spread and spread. Many important industries are directly dependent upon one another. For example, if new car sales are down, the automotive industry will need less steel. The steel industry will slow down, which will mean that it will need less coal for its furnaces, and so on.

To give you a larger appreciation for the extent of interdependence among American industries, let's look at what happened to the home-building industry a few years ago. Demand for new homes declined sharply, principally because prices rose to the point where many potential buyers simply couldn't afford them. Homebuilders reduced their activities, which meant that they cut down their purchases of lumber, affecting the lumber business; cut down their purchases of nails, affecting the steel industry; cut down their purchases of glass, affecting the glass industry; and so on. Since the purchase of new homes was down, the furniture industry was hurt, as were carpet manufacturers, and every other industry that depended on new home purchases for a large part of its normal activity.

ECONOMIC BOOM

While recession is the bottom of the business cycle, the opposite extreme is a **boom.** There is a danger in this extreme, too, because of the ever-present threat of inflation. As we mentioned earlier, when demand exceeds supply, competition for that supply tends to force prices up. When a supplier's prices rise in such a situation, it does not necessarily mean that the supplier is exhibiting unvarnished greed in taking advantage of the situation. There may be another consideration. If production facilities are running at full capacity, and demand for the products is still strong, the supplier will be thinking about expansion of the business. Expansion is financed from profits. Higher prices may mean higher profits, thus making it easier to expand.

Inflationary pressures always tend to increase in an economy that is moving too fast. The economists call it an **over-heated economy.**

CAUSES OF INFLATION

There are three basic causes of inflation, and economists have a phrase for each of them: **cost-push, demand-pull,** and **currency debasement.** The first two terms are highly descriptive if you think of costs pushing prices from below and demand pulling prices from above.

Currency debasement is simply the process of creating new money without a similar increase in the amount of goods or services that can be purchased with that money. Thus, there is more money to be spent, but nothing more to spend it on. This process results in more demand for a given amount of goods and services, and thus higher prices. Governments in the past have tried creating new money by keeping the printing presses running, usually with disastrous economic results.

In the 1970s we have seen both cost-push and demand-pull inflation at work, although not always at the same time. Late in 1972, the economy started coming out of the recession that had begun in 1969—and it came out with a vengeance. Rather than slowly picking up steam, as the economy normally does on the upward wave of the business cycle, it chugged into high gear very quickly.

There was a reason for this peculiar behavior, and it has to do with something called **capacity.** It means, very simply, the maximum amount of product that can be turned out by a production facility. Every factory has a certain capacity. Working at full steam, it can produce just so much of whatever is being manufactured there. Increasing a factory's capacity means expansion, and that can take years to accomplish. For example, if a steel company wanted to expand—by building a new factory or adding on to an old one—it would have to plan on a two- or three-year interval between the official go-ahead and the day the new facility started producing steel.

A good part of the time lag owes to the fact that many agencies of the federal, state, and local governments must grant approval before a steel company (and other primary manufacturers, such as those in chemicals, aluminum, paper, rubber, and such) can proceed to construction of a new facility.

In the late 1960s the expansion rate of many primary manufacturers slowed down. Many of them made very little addition to capacity between 1969 and 1972. Thus, when the economy started heating up again in 1972 and 1973, many primary manufacturers found they didn't have the capacity to meet a surge of new demand.

The paper industry is a good example. Demand for various types of paper began picking up in late 1972 and continued in 1973. Demand was further increased by an artificial stimulus; many of the major users of paper, fearing that they might not be able to get enough to cover their needs, ordered extra supplies for stockpiling. Demand was severely inflated, with several consequences.

First, true to the law of supply and demand, prices rose sharply as users bid aggressively against one another. Secondly, the paper companies cut back on production of lower grades of paper, in order to increase production of the more expensive and more profitable kinds that were in particularly strong demand. This also had an inflationary effect, because it forced many companies that had previously used low-grade paper to buy more expensive grades, the higher costs of which they had to pass on to their customers.

Most of the inflation that we experienced in the 1970s is, however, of the cost-push variety. There is a vicious circle to this kind of inflation that can be very difficult to break. Manufacturers' costs rise, and they pass the costs along to their customers, ultimately pushing up the prices of food, clothing, housing, and other staples of life. Workers, seeing this, react by demanding higher wages. Companies increase wages and then pass along the higher costs, which in turn raises the prices workers must pay for basics. Unless something happens, the circle can grow wider and wider.

WAGE AND PRICE CONTROLS

If the vicious circle is such a serious problem, you might ask, why doesn't the government enforce **wage and price controls**—in other words, limit by law the amounts of increases that may be taken. Economists disagree over the wisdom of this tactic. Those who favor wage and price controls say that such controls would impose stability upon a bad situation that just tends to get worse. Those economists who oppose wage and price controls say that controls can create very serious distortions in the economy—by discouraging business expansion or by encouraging **black-market** sales of products in strong demand—that is, sales at inflated prices that are unrecorded and outside the proper channels.

Though economists disagree over the advisability of wage and price controls, they are in full agreement on one point—that our ability to cope with, and perhaps control, business cycles and inflation depends upon knowing as much as is possible about the condition of our economy at any given time.

The United States has better systems for providing such information than any other country in the world. Most of the truly important economic data are gathered by various agencies of the federal government.

GROSS NATIONAL PRODUCT

The Commerce Department, for example, keeps track of a key indicator of economic health called the gross national product (or simply GNP). The gross national product is the total value of all the goods and services produced in the United States. It is not calculated precisely to the dollar by any means, but it represents a good, solid estimate of what the country has produced. The figure is reported by the Commerce Department four times a year, for each of the annual quarters.

The GNP on an annual basis, incidentally, is currently in the area of $2 *trillion,* an almost incomprehensible figure that if written out in numbers would be a 2 followed by twelve 0's.

Keeping track of the GNP is very important for economists because it tells them whether or not the economy is meeting its growth goals. If, for example, it is believed that a 5 percent rate of growth is healthy

[28]

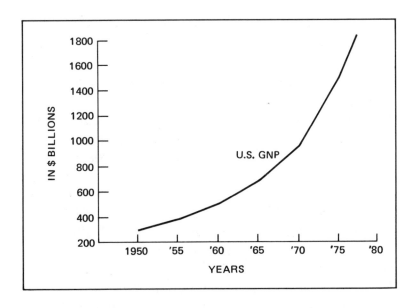

**The American Gross National
Product has risen dramatically.**

from one quarter of the year to another, and the GNP figure reveals a growth rate of, say, 4 percent, the economists are going to get a little worried. The economy is not as healthy as it perhaps should be. If the quarterly figure showed, say, an 8 percent growth rate, economists would worry that it might be growing too fast, suggesting the danger of overheating.

GNP growth rarely comes out exactly as most economists predict it will; as a result, economists tend to worry a lot.

PRICE INDEXES

Two more critically important statistics—the **consumer price index** and the **wholesale price index**—are cal-

[29]

culated by the Labor Department on a monthly basis. Both statistics indicate how much prices have risen from one month to the next.

Both statistics are arrived at in basically the same manner. For the consumer price index, the Labor Department's Bureau of Labor Statistics actually sends people out in various parts of the country and has them buy items on a list of the same 400 products each month. The prices are reported to the Bureau, which calculates from that information how much prices have changed month to month. The consumer price index, or CPI as it is called, is particularly important in that it affects the wages of millions of Americans. Many labor contracts specify that workers' wages must be increased by whatever percentage increase is reported in the CPI.

The wholesale price index is especially important from the economists' point of view. The Bureau gathers the information for this statistic by obtaining current prices on products that are either used in manufacturing or are one or more steps away from sale to the consumer—raw food that is going to be canned, for example. This index sometimes provides an early warning of substantial price increases yet to be felt by the consumer—although it is not consistently an early warning signal.

UNEMPLOYMENT RATE

Another Labor Department index is the **unemployment rate.** The Bureau of Labor Statistics sends part-time employees out once a month to conduct door-to-door surveys of about 47,000 homes in the United States. One of the questions they ask is whether anyone in the household is looking for employment. The Bureau counts as

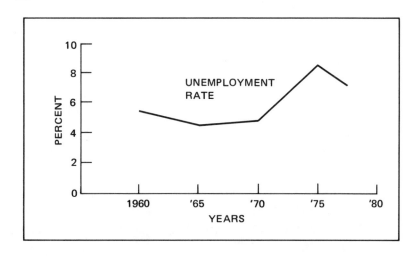

unemployed anyone in the survey households who has been unable to find a job in the previous four weeks.

Although the unemployment rate is considered a very important indicator of economic conditions, it has many critics among business people and economists. Because the figure is arrived at by a door-to-door survey, its accuracy is questioned. On the one hand, it tends to count as unemployed those persons who may not really be looking for a permanent position, but rather one that they will stay with until they have earned a certain amount of money. On the other hand, it does not count as unemployed those who were looking for employment, were unable to find anything, and just gave up.

The unemployment rate is important in many respects, but perhaps its most immediate impact is that when unemployment reaches a certain level in some areas, government assistance funds are made available to local governments in the millions of dollars.

The unemployment rate has a special, though perhaps peculiar, significance as an economic indicator. It is peculiar because many economists worry about the unemployment rate falling too low, but they disagree on how low is too low. Some say 4 percent, some say 3 percent, whatever. What they are saying, in effect, is that there is a desirable level of unemployment.

They are not being heartless about the unemployed; economists are supposed to be unemotional about economic issues. There is a desirable level of unemployment from their point of view because if we had 100 percent employment—if everyone who wanted a job could have one—the threat of serious inflation would rear its ugly head.

Think about it a moment in terms of the law of supply and demand that we spoke of earlier. If everyone were fully employed, where would a company get additional employees when it needed them? It would have to recruit them from other companies. That would create the type of bidding competition that Adam Smith spoke about.

Such a bidding competition for workers would drive wages up, add to the cost of production, and feed inflation. That's what economists mean when they talk about a desirable level of unemployment—a sufficiently large percentage to keep supply and demand forces in balance.

Unemployment, at any level, has its costs beyond the obvious human suffering that it causes. A certain amount of production, consumption, and growth is lost, and the state, local, and federal governments lose tax revenues that are needed to maintain their various public programs.

Unemployment, for many reasons, is the sad shortcoming of our free enterprise economy.

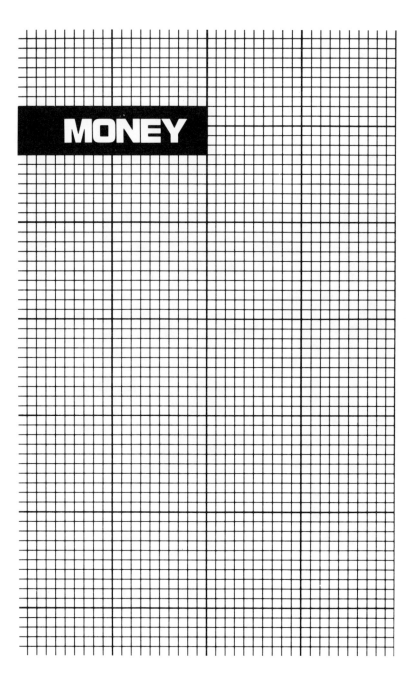

If you ask someone you know to define what **money** is, you are liable to get a quizzical look in return for your question, and a reply something like, "Everyone knows what money is."

If you ask the same question of an economist, you'll probably get an entirely different reaction. People who are supposed to know something about money are usually reluctant to answer such a question with a simple reply. 2065854

What we're saying is that the subject of money is far, far more complicated than it may seem. Perhaps you'd ask, "But isn't this money?" as you pull a dollar bill out of your pocket. Well, yes and no.

If that seems confusing, consider this. There is right now slightly over $100 billion of U.S. currency in circulation. That may seem like a lot, but divide that by the American population of approximately 220 million persons. You'll find that if total currency in circulation were divided equally among the population, each of us would receive less than $500.

Consider this, too. The total amount of money in checking and savings accounts at U.S. commercial banks currently amounts to more than $500 billion. That means that if every person and every business with a checking or savings account attempted to convert it to cash at the same time, there wouldn't be enough currency to go around—not by a wide margin.

Cash, or currency, is not really critically needed for the operation of our economy. It is, in effect, actually just a convenience. Multibillion-dollar corporations conduct their businesses year-in and year-out without handling as much as a dollar in cash. They pay their workers and their suppliers by check; the goods they produce are paid for by check. For many such companies, cash represents an undesirable inconvenience, because it requires a security system to protect it.

In theory, we have the means today to do away with cash altogether. In practice, however, cash will probably never become strictly a museum curiosity.

ELECTRONIC FUNDS TRANSFER

But in the future we will probably be able to sharply reduce the amount of currency we require for the proper operation of our economic system, and eliminate the check-writing system, too. The means for accomplishing these objectives is called the **electronic funds transfer system (EFT,** for short).

This is the way it would work. Every person would have an identification card and a bank account. If someone purchased something in a department store, for example, the salesperson would place the buyer's identification card in a computer terminal and indicate the price of the transaction. The central computer system would deduct the amount of the purchase from the buyer's account and credit it to the store's account immediately.

The same system could be used just as efficiently for transactions between businesses, and for the payment of individuals' monthly bills for such expenses as telephone and electric service and rent or mortgage charges. The system is in fact being used already, in somewhat limited ways, in some parts of the country.

The system's principal limitation, and the reason it will probably not entirely eliminate cash, is in the area of small transactions. Using it for the purchase of something as inexpensive as a newspaper wouldn't be very efficient. Every transaction in an EFT system has a processing cost. That cost generally would be about the same for each transaction, whether it be for a million dollars or 25 cents. It wouldn't make much sense from the point of view of efficiency to burden the system with a lot of 25-cent transactions.

THE PURPOSE OF MONEY

At this point, it would be of some value to consider why money exists at all. What purpose does it actually serve? We mentioned before that money is basically a convenience, and that is precisely why it came into being—to simplify the process of exchanging goods among people.

Far back in history, when people became social beings living in communities, it became convenient to exchange goods. Hunters, for example, found that they could trade the meat their family didn't need for something else that the hunter perhaps couldn't provide—wood for the family's fire, for example.

All goods or services have a certain value. Hunters exchanging a day's supply of meat for a day's supply of wood might not have cared that they had to work harder for their end of the bargain than the wood gatherers did. But as society became more complex, this consideration took on greater importance.

Eventually, the primitive **barter system** of economics had to give way to something a little more sophisticated. Various goods had to develop specific values, otherwise some workers would benefit to the disadvantage of others. Take the hunter and the wood gatherer, for instance. If the hunter took four hours to get enough meat to exchange for a day's supply of wood, and the wood gatherer took half as long to meet the hunter's needs, the hunter was clearly at a disadvantage.

[37]

In primitive societies, the value of certain goods tended to relate very closely to the amount of labor required to obtain or produce them. Once values were established for the goods exchanged by primitive people, certain problems arose in transactions. Basically, it came down to the question (in today's terminology) of how do you make change when the items being offered in exchange have different values and can't be divided up easily?

The solution, of course, was to have the person whose product was of lesser value throw something more into the bargain to satisfy the other party. Whatever was chosen to equalize the transaction (arrowheads, perhaps, but it really doesn't matter), became, in effect, money because it was not an essential part of the bargain, just a convenience to close the exchange.

If certain items were constantly used in this manner, they eventually became symbolic within a primitive community and took on the status of money in the full-fledged sense of the word. Money remains a symbol to this day. Think about it. What is a dollar bill worth? It's only a piece of paper with some printing on it. You can't eat currency; you can't clothe yourself with it. You could burn it if you were cold, but it wouldn't be a very efficient source of fuel.

The fact that money has value comes strictly from what is really an act of faith on the part of society. We believe it has value; therefore, it does have value.

VALUE OF MONEY

But what is the value of money? Theoretically, the sum of money in a society should be equal to the total value of all the goods and services the society produces. Ac-

[38]

tually, those two sides of the equation don't necessarily correspond that closely. Our society and our economic system have become too complicated for that. We can't really know precisely what the value of all goods and services are. (The gross national product is basically only an estimate.) Also, we can't be very exact about the amount of money in the economy. There are reasonably good estimates of the amount of currency in circulation, but, as we pointed out, currency is only a small part of the concept of money.

Nevertheless, estimates of the amount of money in the economy are as important to economists as estimates of the gross national product are. Economists call the basic monetary statistics the **money supply.**

The most closely followed of these figures has come to be known as simply **M-1.** It is a combination of currency in circulation and the amount of money in individual and corporate checking accounts at commercial banks. The statistic is significant because this type of money tends to be turned over relatively quickly. Currency is constantly moving. Most individuals and corporations keep money in checking accounts to meet immediate bills. Since checking accounts in most parts of the country do not pay interest as do savings accounts, it does not make much sense to keep large amounts of money there that could be put to more profitable use.

Since the assumption is that the bulk of M-1 money will be spent in a relatively short period of time, economists watch this figure to get an indication of where the economy is headed in the immediate future, both in terms of business conditions and the trend of prices. Monetary statistics, including M-1, are reported weekly by the **Federal Reserve Board.**

If the growth of M-1 begins to rise, it means that an

increase in spending is likely in the weeks ahead. More money in circulation translates into higher demand for goods and services, which in turn can be inflationary. If the supply of M-1 begins to decline, it suggests that the amount of spending for goods and services will shrink in the immediate future, slackening demand for goods and services and easing inflationary pressures.

To some extent, the growth of M-1 can be controlled, although how much and how well is a matter of sharp disagreement among economists. Before we discuss that, it would be well to take a look at the role of the banks in the economy and explain what the Federal Reserve Board does.

If you wish to even begin to fathom what the banking system is all about, you must understand one fact first—banks exist for the purpose of lending money. Period. Dismiss from your mind any other notions of what a bank is, and you'll find the concept easier to comprehend. Banks make profits from charging borrowers a higher rate of interest than they pay to depositors.

Banks are in a most unusual position (which they share with no less an institution than the U.S. government) of being able to create money. When someone makes a deposit in a savings account, a bank has more money to lend, which it does as quickly as possible, because it must pay interest to the depositor from the day the money is carried through the front door.

When a bank lends a depositor's money, the act more or less creates new money. The borrower has money to use, and the depositor has a claim on it as well, with the right to withdraw it at any time.

This ability to create money has a danger built into it. If the banks exercised this ability too freely, it could put too much money into circulation at one time, which could throw the supply and demand equation out of balance on the demand side. This could overheat the economy and cause a surge of inflation.

FEDERAL RESERVE BOARD

To prevent this from happening, and to control the rate at which banks lend money, Congress established a system of bank controls. The keystone of the system is the Federal Reserve Board. The Board has responsibility for keeping some balance in bank lending policies, with an eye to their impact on the general economy.

The Federal Reserve Board, incidentally, is independent of the other branches of the federal government. Congress, in its infinite wisdom, decided that the Board should not be under the control of the administrative or the legislative branch of the federal government. If that were the case, in view of the impact that the Board has on business conditions, it might be tempting for a President or Congress to try to influence business conditions in an election year. The President does appoint the Board's directors and its chairperson, but once they are in office they cannot be removed until their terms expire. They are free to function without political pressure.

MONEY SUPPLY CONTROL

The Federal Reserve Board controls bank lending policies by expanding or contracting the amount of money the banks have to lend. It would be inappropriate, not to mention unfair, for any agency to tell a bank it couldn't lend depositors' money when the bank is obliged to pay interest on that money. If that were the case, the banks would be caught in a financial squeeze.

What the Federal Reserve Board does is to make use of **U.S. Treasury securities** it holds. If it feels the banks are lending money too quickly, it sells U.S. Treasury securities (which pay interest) for funds that would otherwise go to borrowers. If the Board feels that bank lending is too slow, it buys U.S. Treasury securities, thus putting more lending money at the banks' disposal. The money the Board receives when it sells Treasury securities has no impact on the economy, since the money is retained in the Federal Reserve System.

This procedure directly affects the nation's money supply, and the M-1 figure. When the Board is buying Treasury securities and expanding the amount of money banks have to lend, the funds go out to borrowers and show up in their bank accounts.

No discussion of money could possibly be complete without some reference to **interest rates** and how they are determined.

Basically, the lending and borrowing of money operate under the law of supply and demand. Money is essentially a product just like steel or automobiles as far as the marketplace is concerned. Some people have it and are willing to sell it; some people need it and are willing to buy it. Money has a price, as any other product does, except that in this case it is called interest.

When the demand for money exceeds the supply, interest rates tend to rise. Conversely, when demand is lower than supply, the reverse tends to happen; interest rates drop. These tendencies contribute very positively to helping keep the economy in balance. As demand for money for business expansion rises, pushing up interest rates, the higher rates have a sobering effect on demand. When rates are low because of slack demand, borrowing is encouraged, putting money into a stagnant economy.

There is one major factor outside the supply and demand equation that can affect the level of interest rates quite on its own, and that is inflation. When inflation is high, those who have money to lend look for interest rates that will protect their capital. If you are lending money at a 6 percent rate for a year and the economy suffers an 8 percent inflation rate during that year, the value of your capital has decreased. In other words, the money the lender gets back will purchase less in the way of goods and services than on the day he or she lent it. Let's say the loan amounted to $100. At the end of the year, the lender would get $106 back. But by then, it would take $108 to buy what $100 could purchase on the day the loan was made. That is why high interest rates usually go hand-in-hand with high inflation.

The interest rates banks pay for savings deposits are as much subject to the law of supply and demand as are the rates they charge their borrowers. When banks need money to meet rising loan demand, their principal source of funds is deposit money. To encourage more deposits, they raise interest rates on savings accounts. When loan demand is falling, the banks have less need of deposits, and interest rates are reduced.

DISCOUNT AND PRIME RATES

The banks have one other major source of funds for their lending activities—the Federal Reserve System. They can borrow money from the Federal Reserve, but of course they have to pay a price—an interest charge that is known as the **discount rate.** This provides the Federal

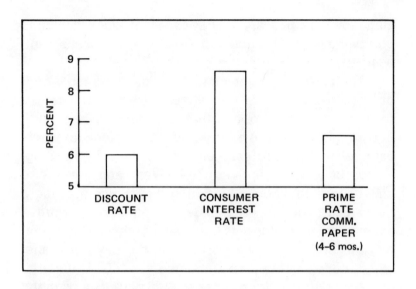

Interest rates are quite different, depending upon who is borrowing.

Reserve with yet another opportunity to control bank lending policies. The Federal Reserve Board raises and lowers the discount rate to suit economic conditions.

Another important phrase relative to bank lending practices is **prime rate.** The prime rate is the interest rate banks charge to their corporate borrowers with the highest credit rating. The rate is changed by the banks to reflect the rates the banks must pay to get money for lending purposes.

The prime rate is an important economic indicator because it will affect the borrowing inclinations of the nation's largest and most important corporations. When the rate is changed, usually one or two banks will take

[44]

the lead in announcing their decision, and others will follow. Except when changes are taking place, the prime rate is normally about the same at all major commercial banks.

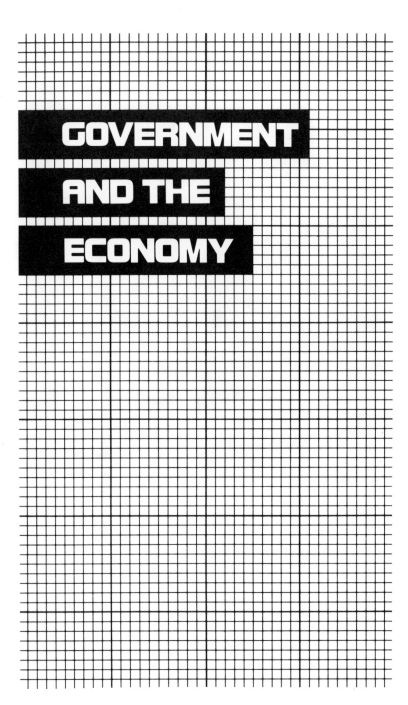

GOVERNMENT AND THE ECONOMY

The most important economist of the twentieth century, without question, was an Englishman named John Maynard Keynes. (His name, incidentally, is pronounced like *canes*.) Although some economists today do not agree with his overall theories, at least in their application, Lord Keynes's thinking has dominated economic theory since the mid-1930s.

Lord Keynes's principles are extremely complex, but they are based on one relatively simple concept—that national governments can, and should, use their spending, taxing, and borrowing powers to alter the course of the economy.

Although this theory is part of common economic practice today in all the major industrial nations, when it was first proposed in the 1930s by Lord Keynes it was considered radical by most economists of the time. In the first place, before World War II, governments played a far smaller role in economic life than today. In the second place, at the time Lord Keynes's theories were first expounded, the economy was considered by most economists to be outside the realm of government interference. Government taxing and borrowing powers were widely viewed in the simplest possible fashion, as solely a means to provide money for the operation of government programs.

THE GREAT DEPRESSION

It was the Great Depression of the 1930s that provided an opportunity to test Keynesian economic theories. After the stock market crash in October 1929, the economies of the major western nations, particularly the United States, fell into decline.

It is important to note that the stock market crash

John Maynard Keynes

of 1929 did not *cause* the Great Depression, as is commonly believed. The signs of a very serious economic downturn were visible months before the crash. The crash, however, probably made the Depression worse than it might have been otherwise, because it severely eroded the public's confidence in business, and in the economy in general.

After the Depression set in, most economists of the day correctly viewed the situation as largely a crisis of confidence. The public and businesses were not spending money because they had lost faith in the system. Thus, in the very early days of the Depression, the effort to restore economic health revolved around public comments by well-known business and political leaders, expressing confidence that everything was going to be all right.

With the benefit of hindsight, that might seem to have been an almost pathetic way to try to put the economy back in order, but under less severe circumstances it might have been successful.

Of course, it didn't work. Although the economy showed occasional signs of perking up in the early 1930s, improvements were invariably short-lived. Conditions gradually worsened. At the height of the Great Depression, around 1935, fully 25 percent of American workers were unemployed, and an additional large percentage were not working on a full-time basis.

One of Lord Keynes's principal recommendations at the time was that governments borrow money to stimulate their economies. The principle is common enough today. When a government spends more money than it takes in in taxes, a deficit is created. To fill the gap, the government borrows money. This means that money is taken from the future (when the borrowing will actually be repaid) and put into circulation now. This practice adds to the money supply, which means more spending now for goods and services.

The U.S. government adopted Lord Keynes's recommendation in the 1930s in an effort to stimulate the economy. Unfortunately, it was not as successful an endeavor as its proponents had hoped it would be. Keynesian economists, however, believe that it was done on too small a scale to be fully successful in the 1930s in view of how severe and deeply ingrained the Great Depression was.

By a sad and ironic twist, it was World War II that finally brought the Depression to an end. Even before the United States entered the war, American business was gearing up to provide war material for the Allied countries. The enormous cost of the war-production effort was largely financed by massive U.S. government borrowing, which was in reality a major application of Keynesian economics.

Lord Keynes's economic principles apply to government taxing and spending policies as well as borrowing practices. The government can deeply affect the economy by the amount of taxes it levies and by the timing of its expenditures.

TAXES AND THE ECONOMY

For example, if the economy is overheating, an increase in taxes will reduce the money supply, taking funds out of the economic system and thus slowing down demand for goods and services. When the economy is slack, a tax reduction will have the opposite effect.

If the government, which spends over $500 billion

a year (representing the equivalent of about one-quarter of the gross national product), delays spending even a few billion dollars for a few months, it will also slow down the economy by reducing the money supply. Thus, the government is capable of manipulating the economy in a number of different ways.

We mentioned earlier that some economists do not agree with Lord Keynes's economic theories. To be more specific, no one doubts the government's ability to affect the economy by its actions. Opponents of Keynesian economics question whether the government *should* be playing this role in the economy and whether there isn't a more efficient means of achieving economic stability.

Probably the best known exponent of the contrary view is Professor Milton Friedman of the University of Chicago. Professor Friedman and his followers feel that the proper place for control of the money supply, and hence control of the economy, is the Federal Reserve Board.

Basically, Professor Friedman believes that the government's reactions to economic problems are too slow and cumbersome and often misguided. For example, if the economy is moving slowly and a tax cut is considered to be the appropriate means of stimulating it, the process of having the President draw up a tax-cut proposal and getting Congressional approval can take months. In the meantime, the economy might be well on its way to correcting itself, and the tax cut might come at a time when the economy does not need that kind of stimulation. Professor Friedman also feels that because the government is so massive and has so large an impact on the economy, its reactions to economic problems tend to be overwhelming and shouldn't be trusted; that is, if economic stimulus is desired, the government's solutions tend to overstimulate the economy.

Professor Friedman believes that the Federal Reserve Board, since its objectives can be more narrowly focused, is in a better position to fine-tune the economy. Those who disagree with the Friedman view, however, claim that it is difficult, if not impossible, to control the money supply as carefully as a well-balanced economy requires, and that even if it were possible, monetary controls alone would not be effective.

All efforts to control the money supply are confronted by conflicting economic forces—inflation on the one side, and recession on the other. If the rate of growth of the money supply is increased to avoid recession, too fast a growth can result in accelerating inflation. Conversely, if, to avoid inflation, growth of the money supply is constricted, the threat of recession can arise.

In some situations, economists can be faced with the dilemma of having to choose between the lesser of evils. Where serious inflation is in progress, which calls for correction, the alternative of constricting the growth in money supply is a gamble that the country could lapse into a recession.

ECONOMIC "STAGFLATION"

In this respect, the science of economics has been complicated in recent years by a peculiar condition that the economists have come to call **stagflation.** For a long time, it was the conventional wisdom in economics that inflation and a stagnant economy could not exist simultaneously for very long. Unfortunately, we have

**Milton Friedman received the
1976 Nobel Prize for Economics.**

had exactly that combination of forces in the U.S. economy over the past few years. Economists, seldom at a loss for words, put the two supposedly conflicting terms together as a short-hand method of describing the phenomenon.

Since we're on the subject of terminology, the question might naturally be asked, What constitutes a recession, and how does it differ from a **depression?**

Well, that depends on which economist you ask. Different economists may define both terms differently. Some economists would say that we are in a recession if the unemployment rate exceeds 6 percent, and in a depression if it passes 10 percent. Others define a recession as three consecutive quarters of declining growth in the gross national product, and a depression as when the gross national product itself is in decline over a period of time.

The terms used for economic slowdowns have been changing over the years. Economist John Kenneth Galbraith in *Money: Whence It Came, Where It Went,* one of his many books, offers a witty explanation for the succession of terms used.

> *During the last century and until 1907, the United States had panics, and that, unabashedly, is what they were called. But, by 1907, language was becoming, like so much else, the servant of economic interest. To minimize the shock to confidence, businessmen and bankers had started to explain that any current economic setback was not really a panic, only a crisis. . . . By the 1920's, however, the word* crisis *had also acquired the fearsome connotation of the event it described. Accordingly, men offered reassurance by explaining that it was not a*

crisis, only a depression. A very soft word. Then the Great Depression associated the most frightful of economic misfortunes with that term, and economic semanticists now explained that no depression was in prospect, at most only a recession. In the 1950's, when there was a modest setback, economists and public officials were united in denying that it was a recession—only a sidewise movement or a rolling readjustment.

But what about the role of the **stock market** in the American economy? If you look back at the history of the stock market, you will find that it often declines just before the country suffers an economic setback, whether it was called a depression or a recession. From that, it would be rational to conclude that the stock market and economic setbacks have a close relationship—almost a cause-and-effect relationship, in fact.

The stock market, unfortunately, has gotten much unjustified blame for causing economic downturns. Except for its psychological impact on people's willingness to spend money, which can worsen or extend a recession, the stock market is entirely neutral in its economic contributions.

The stock market actually is an *indicator* of economic conditions, a sort of signal that shows how much confidence the public has in the economy. And it is as reliable an indicator as the other indexes we have referred to previously—the unemployment rate, the consumer price index, the gross national product.

The stock market is, in fact, the closest thing we have to a meaningful public opinion poll of confidence in the economy. That is precisely why it tends to decline *before* economic setbacks occur; the public begins to

**Another hectic day on the floor
of the New York Stock Exchange.**

perceive that something is wrong with the economy even before the signs are necessarily apparent to the economists.

STOCKS AND BONDS

There are enough widespread misconceptions about **stocks** and **bonds** and the world of Wall Street to warrant a few words here on just what it is all about.

To begin with, stocks and bonds are two entirely different creatures. One way to differentiate is to think of a stock as a share of ownership, and a bond as a borrowing. When you have stocks, you are a part owner in a company. When you have bonds, you are a lender; some institution has borrowed money from you with the promise that you will be paid back with interest.

When stocks are traded on the market, it means that shares of ownership are changing hands. The money you pay to purchase a stock does not go to the company whose shares you buy; it goes to the previous owner. The only time a company sees any money from the sale of its stock is when it sells what is called a **new issue,** and such sales are very clearly indicated as such.

Well, why do stock prices go up and down, and why do they reflect perceptions of the health of the economy?

In the first place, the trading of stocks is one of the activities in our modern complex society where you can still see the law of supply and demand at work in its purest form.

Stocks go up in price when the demand for them is greater than the supply; that is, when potential buyers are more interested in purchasing than owners of stock are in selling. Turn the equation around and you'll understand why prices go down.

But what motivates the buyers and sellers? That is not an easy question to answer. Basically, the buyer of stock assumes that later on someone will be willing to pay more for his or her shares than it cost the buyer to obtain them. Underlying this is the fact that if the economy is healthy and the company whose shares are purchased is a good one, the company will prosper and the owners will share in the company's good fortune. Conversely, if the economy goes sour, it will likely be more difficult for the company to do well, and the underlying value of its stock will diminish.

COMMODITIES

The **commodities markets**—where wheat, corn, cattle, and the like are sold—operate in a fashion similar to the stock market. The prices go up and down in response to supply and demand factors. If demand is constant and supply drops (if bad weather reduces the wheat crop, for example) the price of a commodity will rise. Conversely, if demand is constant and supply of a commodity is greater than anticipated, the price will drop.

A few years ago, when food prices rose sharply, the commodities markets drew a lot of unfair criticism for their role in the price increases. It was unfair because they reflect not what some group of persons wants them to reflect, but the balance of supply and demand.

The production of food is very different from the production of finished goods in our modern, free-enterprise economy in that supplies of any kind of food product are subject to many variables. Theoretically, the manufacturer of finished goods (a radio, for example) could withhold products from the market, reducing the supply, and, if demand held up, could throw the supply-

The commodities market has its own special method of operation.

demand equation out of balance, with the possibility of higher prices. The competition, of course, would tend to discourage that. More importantly, the manufacturer has an investment in a factory and equipment that must be paid for. It would be disadvantageous not to produce.

The growing of food is a different matter. The manufacturer first determines all of the costs, and then prices the products accordingly, allowing some margin for profit. The wheat farmer, for example, can't work that way. The farmer's prices are determined by supply and demand factors that are largely out of the farmer's control. There is no idea at the time the crop is planted either how much will be produced (the weather will control that), or what prices will be.

Is there a better way to price raw food products to protect the grower and guarantee some profit? No one has found one yet, but in the long run, supply and demand factors tend to work out any imbalances in the system. If farmers aren't getting enough money for their products, they are inclined to plant less, or to switch to more profitable crops.

TWO KEY ECONOMIC SYSTEMS

Since we were discussing the government's ability to alter the course of the economy, it would seem appropriate to take a look here at the two basic systems of economics in the world—the **capitalist system,** such as we have in the United States, and the **communist system,** such as exists in the Soviet Union.

The word *capitalist* as applied to our system in comparison with that of the Soviet Union is not altogether correct. Both systems require capital for functioning. Without it, there would be no possibility of growth—in the capitalist *or* communist economies. The major difference between us in this respect is the source of capital. In our system, it comes basically from individuals; in the Soviet system, it comes from the government, which owns the means of production.

Aside from this, there is one very significant difference between our systems—and that is in the determination of what will be produced, how much will be produced, and what the prices will be.

Our **free enterprise system** leaves the determination to the markets—in effect, to the public. Supply will be established by demand.

In the communist system of economics, supply is established by government decree. The state attempts to plan what the market will get. The rulers of the Soviet Union attempt to suspend the law of supply and demand. This can have some unfortunate results. If public demand grows quickly for a particular product, the government must respond to that demand before supplies can be increased. If it is slow to respond, and demand remains high, a black market (outside the normal channels of exchange) springs up and prices react in the normal supply and demand equation.

The communist system of planning is flawed in that it is impossible for a few people who must make the decisions on supply to accurately gauge what the public will demand in the way of goods and services.

Our system, too, has its flaws, but it tends to react much more quickly to what the public wants. The principal flaw is that public demand for any goods and services rises and falls in a free enterprise economy. As a result, we suffer ups and downs in our economic system.

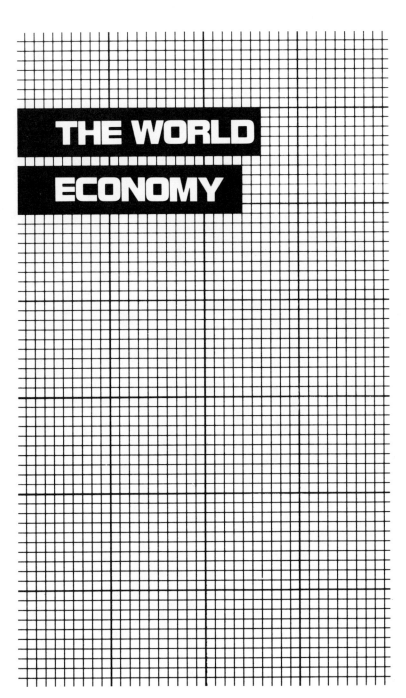

THE WORLD ECONOMY

If the economy of the United States operated all by itself, independently of any other nation, correcting our problems would be a far easier task than it is. Unfortunately, we cannot isolate ourselves from the rest of the world economically any more than we can wave a magic wand and whisk ourselves back to the quieter, simpler life-style of the early 1900s.

The world's economic problems have become our problems, and vice-versa. In the past several years, the United States has experienced many economic difficulties that are directly attributable to the world economy and its relationship with ours. In 1977, the value of the U.S. dollar dropped sharply in comparison with the currencies of other major industrial nations. Rising imports of oil, together with higher prices demanded by foreign countries for their crude oil, have put many billions of our dollars into the hands of foreign interests.

The question is, How are we hurt by events such as these?

That requires a look at some of the key elements of international trade and their relationships to one another. Let's begin with the basic index of a country's economic health relative to the rest of the world—the **balance of payments,** or **BOP.**

BOP, as it is known in economists' short-hand, is a single figure arrived at by comparing the amount of money a country gets for its **exports** (the products it makes for sale in other countries) and the amounts it pays for its **imports** (the products it buys from other countries) over the period of a year. Also calculated into BOP is the amount of money going into or out of a country for other purposes, such as investments. If you subtract one figure from the other, you come up with a surplus or a deficit.

In 1977, the United States suffered a deficit of about $27 billion in its balance of payments, by far the largest such deficit in our history. The year before, for the sake of comparison, the deficit amounted to $5.7 billion.

Why so large a negative figure? Imported oil was the principal cause. We imported $45 billion worth of it in 1977. Looking toward the future, that is an ominous figure, because for many years we have been importing increasingly larger percentages of the oil we need. In 1977, 47.1 percent of our domestic oil demand was met with imports. The year before, it was 41.8 percent.

Well, what difference does it make where we get our oil as long as we get enough for our own needs? There is a chain of reasons why it makes a big difference for the health of our economy. First of all, if our oil imports were halved, we might have shown a surplus in our balance of payments for 1977. As it is, we left $27 billion more of our money overseas than was there at the beginning of 1977. That is $27 billion that could have been circulating in our own economy and stimulating it.

INTERNATIONAL CURRENCY VALUES

The impact of such sizable deficits is eventually felt in the **international value of the dollar.** Currency on the international market is subject to the old law of supply and demand. When foreigners get dollars for their products, they frequently want to exchange them for their own currency or the currency of another nation. When such exchanges are out of balance in supply and demand terms, the value of the currency in greater supply will drop. And that is precisely what happened to the dollar in the foreign exchange markets in 1977. It bought

DOLLAR VALUE CHANGES (approximate)		
YEAR	JAPAN (YEN)	UNITED STATES
1975	305	$1.00
1976	293	$1.00
1977	278	$1.00
1978	190	$1.00

Each year the dollar buys fewer and fewer yen.

increasingly fewer German marks, or French francs, or Japanese yen. This has several long-range ramifications. First, it does have one positive side. It makes American products less expensive for foreigners to buy, because while U.S. companies continue to price their goods in dollar terms, on translation the prices are reduced for overseas markets. On the other hand, it makes the cost of imported products higher here in the United States.

In the long run, the reduced value of the U.S. dollar hurts the stability of the international trade community. The dollar continues to be the keystone currency of world trade. It is not in the imperious position it once was, but it is still the world's number one currency. Many international trade agreements, particularly between developing countries (those that are not major industrial powers), have trade prices specified in dollars because of worry about the stability of the trading partners' currencies.

GOLD STANDARD

Up until the early 1970s, the American economy was so dominant in the world economy that the dollar was the currency against which the value of all other currencies was established. This was as much due to our economic position in the world as it was to the fact that the U.S. government stood ready to exchange gold at $35 an ounce for the dollars that any foreigner wanted to turn in. The **gold standard,** as it was called, lasted from the mid-1930s until 1971.

The United States was forced off the gold standard by a shrinkage of its stock of gold and by the general realization that it couldn't keep its promises to redeem dollars for gold. The irony is that as long as foreigners really believed the U.S. would back its dollars with gold, there was no reason to do so. If the dollar was as good as gold, who needed gold?

When the dollar was taken off the gold standard, a new system had to be devised for appraising the value of the many national currencies. As a substitute, currencies were permitted to **float** on the foreign exchange markets; that is, their values were to be determined by supply and demand factors.

The international trade community had to build some safeguards into this system to prevent the currency of a nation in economic difficulties from being sold into worthlessness. One of the means of doing this is by having the central banks of the nations whose currency is strong go into the market when one currency is under pressure and offer to buy large volumes of the currency, thus bringing supply and demand factors back into balance.

SWAP AGREEMENT

Another tactic is what is called the **swap agreement.** When the currency of one nation comes under selling pressure, that nation may arrange to borrow large quantities of a currency whose price remains strong, and then use the borrowed currency to buy its own on the markets, thus at least partially equalizing supply and demand forces. The borrower agrees to repay the "loan" in the original currency after the markets stabilize. In January of 1977, a swap agreement between West Germany and the United States helped stabilize the value of the dollar after a serious slide.

The importance of all this maneuvering in the currency markets will have significant bearing on the growth of international trade. Sharp currency fluctuations tend to discourage trade. If a West German company, for example, enters into a contract with a United States firm to deliver a quantity of goods, a price must be agreed upon. But if the value of the U.S. dollar and German mark are constantly fluctuating one against the other, one of the parties takes the risk of suffering a loss.

Let's say that a price is agreed upon in U.S. dollars —say, $100 per unit of product sold. If the value of the dollar drops by 10 percent between the time the contract is signed and the delivery date of the goods, the West German company will get $100 per unit for the sale, but now it will buy only $90 worth of marks on conversion. There are ways the companies can protect themselves, but they involve additional expenses.

IMPORTANCE OF WORLD TRADE

If international trade is such a complicated business, why doesn't the United States simply keep its business at home? One obvious and compelling reason for pushing exports right now is to offset the outflow of dollars being spent for foreign oil. If we stopped exporting and continued bringing in the large quantities of foreign oil we're using, we would be in even worse shape than now.

Secondly, the United States needs its foreign sales for the well-being of the domestic economy. There would be no new markets opening up domestically for many of the products we are most successful at selling abroad. Where would we find new domestic markets, for example, for the many computers and other sophisticated electronic equipment we sell abroad. The jobs of millions of American workers are dependent upon our continuing to sell products and services to other countries of the world.

Thirdly, the United States, which was once almost self-sufficient in raw materials, is slowly exhausting domestic supplies of many of the things we need to remain a modern industrial nation. We are gradually using up our own supplies of oil and natural gas, for example. That is also true of many basic minerals, such as bauxite for the manufacture of aluminum.

The nations of the world are gradually becoming interdependent, that is, they depend upon one another. There is simply no way to reverse this trend, other than to completely change our way of living.

Studies have shown that Americans as a whole have a very poor understanding of economics. This is a most unfortunate situation. In the communist system of economics, there is little need for the people to understand the workings of their economic order because they do not participate in the decisions that determine what sort of standard of living they will have. The government does that for them.

The capitalist system is different. We are all active participants in it. We are economic voters, in a sense. We determine what the system will supply for us by the way in which we spend our money. We determine what will be produced and what will not be produced.

Our system has proved that it can provide the best standard of living for our people. But the greatest danger our economic system faces is ignorance. If enough of us do not understand how the system works, it may not survive.

Thus, better understanding of economics is more than a simple exercise in learning. It is a contribution to the continuance of a way of life.

GLOSSARY

Balance of Payments (BOP) The difference between the amount of money that is transferred out of a country for purchases of goods, investments, and other reasons, and the amount of money that comes in, over a given period of time—usually a year or a quarter of a year. If the amount transferred out exceeds the amount coming in, the country has a deficit in this account, or a negative balance of payments. If the reverse is true, it has a surplus in this account, or a positive balance of payments.

Barter system The practice of exchanging goods without the need for any money changing hands.

Black market The selling of goods outside the normal marketplace. It usually occurs where demand exceeds supply and there are government restrictions on the prices that can be charged for the goods being exchanged.

Bonds An interest-bearing security issued by a borrower to the person from whom the money is being borrowed. The security legally binds the borrower to repay the borrowing with interest.

Boom A rapid expansion of economic activity, usually occurring when all major industries are operating at full speed or close to it.

Business cycle The tendency in the capitalist system for economic activity to rise and fall periodically.

Capacity The practical limit on the amount of goods that can be produced by a factory, a company, or an industry when operating at maximum speed.

Capital The means by which production of goods and services is attained, aside from labor and materials.

Capital intensive A phrase applied to businesses that require large amounts of capital for production of goods.

Capitalist system An economic order in which ownership of the means of production is in private hands.

Commodities markets The centralized marketplace for the exchange of certain goods, usually those produced by agriculture or mining.

Communist system An economic order in which ownership of the means of production is in government hands.

Consumer Price Index (CPI) A survey conducted by the U.S. Department of Labor that keeps track, on a monthly basis, of percentage changes in the cost of living for the general public.

Cost-push inflation An increase in the prices of goods and services caused by rising costs of producing those goods or services.

Currency debasement inflation An increase in the prices of goods and services caused by a deliberate increase in the supply of money without a similar rise in the amount of goods or services produced.

Demand-pull inflation An increase in the prices of goods and services caused by a rising demand for those services, particularly where demand is rising faster than those goods and services can be produced.

Depression A severe decline in economic activity, usually associated with very high rates of unemployment and low utilization of productive facilities.

Discount rate The interest rate banks must pay when borrowing money from the Federal Reserve System.

Dividend The shareholders' share in the profitability of a company.

Division of labor The separation of a production process into different stages, and the assignment of workers to each of those stages for maximum efficiency.

Electronic Funds Transfer system (EFT) A system of accounting for the transmittal of money between buyers and sellers without the need for money changing hands or checks being exchanged.

Exports Goods produced in one country and transferred for sale to another.

Federal Reserve Board The administrative arm of the central banking system of the United States that is responsible principally for the control of the nation's money supply.

Float The system by which the values of various countries' currencies are permitted to rise and fall against one another based mainly on supply and demand factors.

Free enterprise system See *Capitalist system.*

Gold standard The system of supporting the value of currency by the willingness to exchange that currency for a given amount of gold.

Gross national product (GNP) The total value of goods and services produced in a country in a given period of time, most often on a yearly basis.

Imports Goods transferred into a country that have been produced elsewhere.

Inflation The decline in the purchasing power of money, or, just as correctly, the increase in the value of goods and services relative to the value of money.

Interest rate The price paid for borrowing money, usually expressed as a percentage.

International value of dollar The price in other currencies for buying U.S. money. If one were holding British pounds or some other currency and wanted to exchange them for dollars, the amount of foreign currency needed to buy a given amount of dollars would depend on the value set at the time by the international currency markets. Those values are determined by supply and demand—that is, if more people are selling dollars than are buying them, their international value is declining.

Labor intensive A phrase applied to businesses that require large amounts of labor for the production of goods or services.

M-1 The most important money supply figure, composed of money in bank checking accounts and currency in circulation.

Money The valuation system by which goods and services are exchanged in our modern economic system.

Money supply The total amount of money available at any given time in the economic system for the purchase of goods and services.

New issue Stocks or bonds offered for the first time to the investing public, and never previously traded.

"Over-heated" economy An expansion of economic activity that is too strong to be sustained without serious side effects, such as inflation or the threat of sudden reversal.

Prime rate The interest rate banks charge on borrowings by corporations with the very best credit ratings.

Productivity The total national output of goods and services determined on a per-worker basis, and usually used for comparison purposes—one year to the next, or one country to another.

Profit The amount of money left after all the costs of producing goods and services have been subtracted from the selling price.

Real wages The amount of money workers have to spend after all deductions have been made from their total pay. Deductions include all items of a tax nature, such as income and Social Security taxes, unemployment insurance payments, and the like.

Recession A slowing down in the rate of economic activity, usually associated with high unemployment rates and a drop in the utilization of production facilities. (For comparison, see *Depression*.)

Shareholders The owners of a corporation, so called because they hold shares in the company's ownership.

Stagflation A term coined by economists to describe a peculiar economic condition where the economy is stagnant and is simultaneously suffering inflation. Both stagnancy and inflation rarely exist at the same time.

Stock market The place where stocks are exchanged. The

phrase is coming to be less and less applied to an actual location, and has come to mean the process of exchanging stocks.

Stocks Securities of ownership in a corporation. (See *Shareholders.*)

Swap agreement An arrangement between countries, or the central banks of countries, whereby the strong currency of one will be borrowed by the other and used to purchase the borrowing country's currency on the international markets. This helps support the value of the borrowing country's currency when it is being weakened by selling pressures.

Taxes Money taken by a government from individuals and corporations for the support of that government's programs.

Unemployment rate The percentage of people out of work at any given time. It is determined by taking the number who are unable to find work and dividing that figure by the number of people in the workforce, both employed and unemployed.

U.S. Treasury securities Bonds and notes of indebtedness sold by the federal government when it borrows money for its operations.

Wage and price controls Limits established by a government on the amount of money that can be charged for goods or for labor.

Wholesale Price Index A survey conducted by the U.S. Department of Labor that keeps track, on a monthly basis, of price changes for raw materials used in the production of goods, or agricultural products at the wholesaler's level. The index is important because it sometimes provides early warning of impending increases in prices that the consumer must pay.

Working capital Money used for operations of a business, as contrasted with investment capital, which is used to purchase equipment, build facilities, or otherwise acquire the means of production.

RECOMMENDED READING

Brue, Stanley L., and Donald R. Wentworth. *Economic Scenes: Theory in Today's World.* Englewood Cliffs, N.J.: Prentice-Hall, 1976.

Galbraith, John Kenneth. *The Age of Uncertainty.* New York: Houghton Mifflin, 1977.

———. *Money: Whence It Came, Where It Went.* New York: Houghton Mifflin, 1975.

Gemmill, Paul F. *Fundamentals of Economics.* New York: Harper & Row, 1960.

Lynn, Robert A. *Basic Economic Principles.* 3rd ed. New York: McGraw-Hill, 1974.

Malabre, Alfred L., Jr. *Understanding the Economy: For People Who Can't Stand Economics.* New York: Dodd, Mead & Company, 1976.

Silk, Leonard. *Economics in Plain English.* New York: Simon & Schuster, 1978.

BIBLIOGRAPHY

Ashley, William J. *An Introduction to English Economic History and Theory.* Fairfield, N.J.: Augustus M. Kelley, 1966.

Brue, Stanley L., and Donald R. Wentworth. *Economic Scenes: Theory in Today's World.* Englewood Cliffs, N.J.: Prentice-Hall, 1976.

Dowd, Douglas F. *The Twisted Dream: Capitalist Development in the United States Since 1776.* Cambridge, Mass.: Winthrop Publishers, 1973.

Galbraith, John Kenneth. *The Age of Uncertainty.* New York: Houghton Mifflin, 1977.

————. *Money: Whence It Came, Where It Went.* New York: Houghton Mifflin, 1975.

Gemmill, Paul F. *Fundamentals of Economics.* New York: Harper & Row, 1960.

Gitlow, Abraham L. *Economics.* New York: Oxford University Press, 1962.

Horton, Byrne J. *Dictionary of Modern Economics.* Washington, D.C.: Public Affairs Press, 1948.

Lynn, Robert A. *Basic Economic Principles.* 3rd ed. New York: McGraw-Hill, 1974.

Malabre, Alfred L., Jr. *Understanding the Economy: For People Who Can't Stand Economics.* New York: Dodd, Mead & Company, 1976.

Mansfield, Edwin. *Economics: Principles, Problems, Decisions.* New York: W. W. Norton & Company, 1974.

Means, Gardner C., et al. *The Roots of Inflation.* New York: Burt Franklin and Company, 1975.

Samuelson, Paul A. *Economics.* 10th ed. New York: McGraw-Hill, 1976.

Sherman, Howard J. *Elementary Aggregate Economics.* New York: Appleton-Century-Crofts, 1966.

Silk, Leonard S., and Phillip Saunders. *The World of Economics.* New York: McGraw-Hill, 1969.

Smith, Adam. *The Wealth of Nations.* Edited by Andrew Skinner. New York: Penguin Books, 1970.

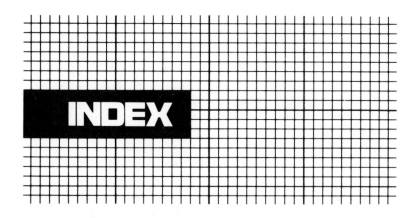

INDEX

Deficit spending, 51–52
Demand
    increasing, 25, 26–27, 28, 40, 59
    slackening, 23–24, 52
Depression, 49–51, 52, 56, 57
Discount rates, 43–44
Dividends, 15
Division of labor, 8–11
Dollar, U.S., 67, 68–70, 71–72

Economic downturn, 51, 56–57
Economic principles and theories, 7, 23, 49
    Friedman's, 53–54
    Keynes's, 49, 51–53
    Smith's, 7–8
Economic systems
    capitalist, 39, 62–63, 73
    communist, 62–63, 73
    primitive, 37–38
Economics, 3, 4, 54, 73
    modern, 7, 8, 49
Economist(s), 3, 4, 23, 25, 31, 32, 35, 39, 51, 52, 54, 56, 57, 59
    disagreement among, 27–28, 49
Economy, the, 16, 17, 21, 28, 35–36, 39, 40, 44
    American, 3, 23, 49, 56, 57, 67, 70
    balance of, 42, 53, 54
    government effect on, 25, 49, 52–54, 62–63
    health of, 11, 59, 60, 68
    over-heated, 25, 29, 41, 52
    stagnant, 43, 54
    stimulation of, 51, 52–54, 68
    world, 3, 67–73

EFT system. *See* Electronic Funds Transfer system
Electronic Funds Transfer system (EFT), 36–37
Employment, high, 23, 32
Expansion, business, 14, 17, 25, 26, 42–43
Exports, 67, 72

Federal Reserve Board, 39, 40, 41–45, 53, 54
"Floating" currencies, 70
Free enterprise system, 15, 21, 23, 32, 60, 63
Friedman, Milton, 53–54
Furniture industry, 24

Galbraith, John Kenneth, 56–57
German mark, 69, 71, 72
Glass industry, 24
GNP. *See* Gross national product
Gold standard, 70–71
Great Depression, the, 49–51, 52, 57
Gross national product (GNP), 3, 11, 28–29, 39, 53, 56, 57

Home building industry, 24

Imports, 67
Industrial Age, the, 7–8
Industrial nations, 49, 67, 72
Industrialization, 8
Inflation, 12, 16, 24, 28, 32, 40, 43, 54
    causes, 21, 25–27, 41
    cost-push, 25, 27
    currency debasement, 25
    demand-pull, 25

Interest
　　on bonds, 59
　　on savings accounts, 39, 40, 41–42, 43
　　on U.S. Treasury securities, 42
Interest rates, 40, 42–43, 44

Job market, 17

Key industries, 24, 26
Keynes, John Maynard, 49, 51, 52, 53

Labor Department, U.S., 30
Labor intensive industries, 14
Lumber industry, 24

Mass production, 8–10, 11
M-1, 39–40, 42
Monetary controls, 54
Monetary statistics, 39
Money, 3, 13, 14, 15, 35–45, 49, 51, 57, 62, 67, 73
　　in circulation, 40, 41, 52
　　creation of, 25
Money supply, the, 3, 39, 42, 52, 53
　　control of, 41–43, 53, 54
Money: Whence It Came, Where It Went (Galbraith), 56–57

Oil imports, 67, 68, 72

Panic(s), 56
Paper industry, 26–27
Pin manufacturing, 8–10, 13
President, the, 41, 53
Price indexes, 29–30
Price trends, 39

Prices, 63, 69
　　declining, 21, 59, 60
　　rising, 3, 12, 15–16, 21, 24–25, 27, 28, 30, 60, 62, 67
Primary (Key) industries, 24, 26
Prime rate, 3, 43–45
Production line, 16
Productivity, 3, 11–16
Profits, 14–17, 25, 40, 62

Recession, 24, 54, 56, 57
　　causes, 21, 23–24
　　(1969), 23, 25
　　(1975), 23
Recovery, economic, 23, 25, 26

Savings accounts, 35, 39, 40
Smith, Adam, 7–10, 21, 32
Soviet Union, 62, 63
Stagflation, 54–55
Standard of living, 10, 12, 15, 73
Steel industry, 14, 24
Stock market, 57–59, 60
　　1929 crash, 49–51
Stocks, 59–60
Supply and demand, 24–25, 43, 60–62, 70
　　balance of, 23, 32, 41, 71
　　law of, 21, 27, 32, 42, 59, 63, 68
Surplus, 67, 68
Swap agreement, 71–72

Taxes, 15, 41, 52–54
Textile industry, 8
Trade, international, 67, 69–70, 71, 72–73
Treasury securities, 42

Unemployment, 23, 31, 32, 51

Unemployment rate, 3, 30–32, 56, 57
United States, 7, 28, 52, 62, 68, 69, 72

Wage and price controls, 27–28
Wages, 12, 14, 15, 16, 27, 30, 32

Wall Street, 59
Wealth of Nations, The (Smith), 7, 8, 21
Wholesale price index, 29–30
Workers, 12, 16, 27, 35, 37, 51, 72
World War II, 49, 52